Loon Summer

Loon Summer

nature poems & wilderness photos

poems by
Yvona Fast

photos by
Nina Schoch.

atmosphere press

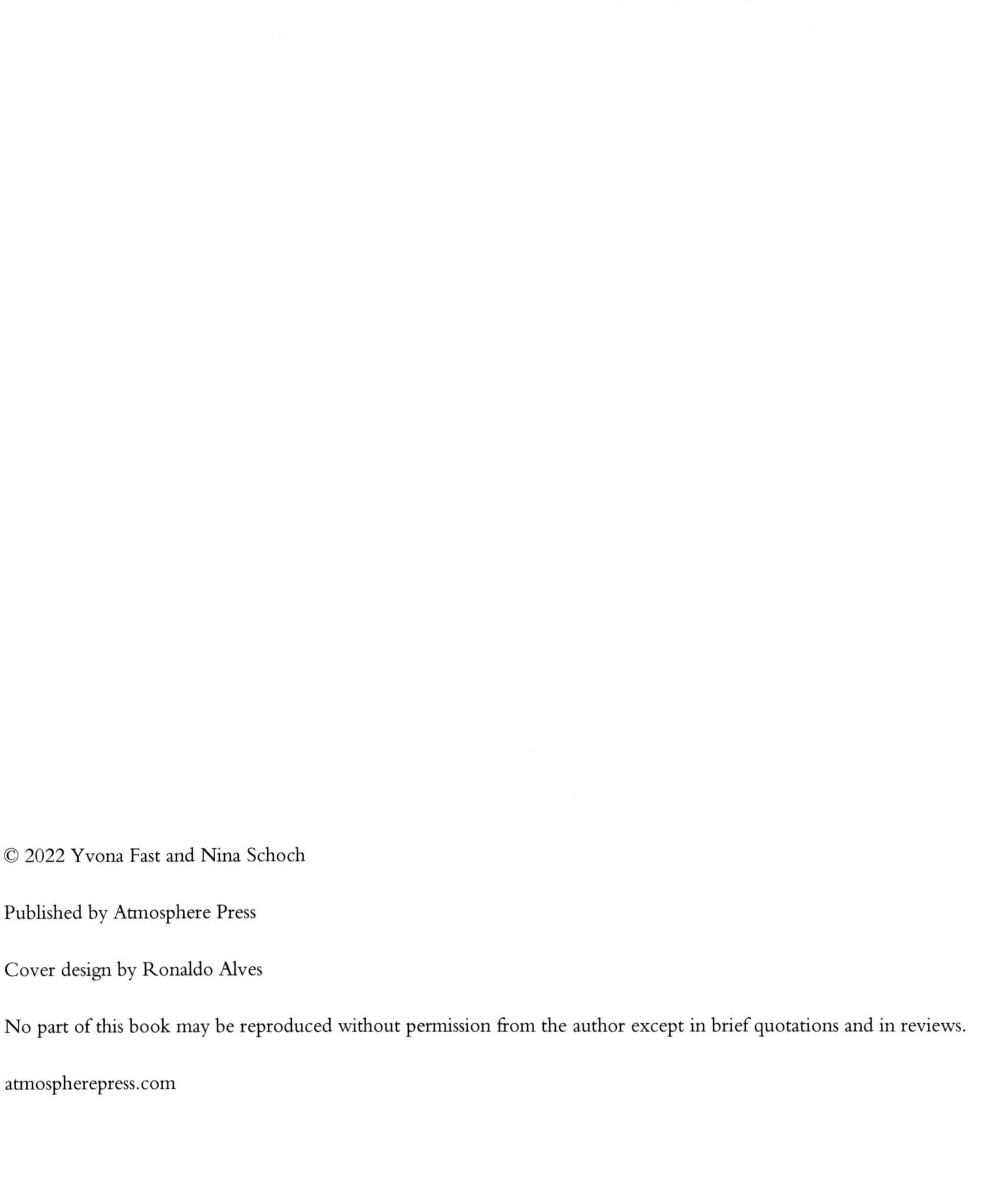

Published by Atmosphere Press

Cover design by Ronaldo Alves

atmospherepress.com

Contents

Waiting 3

Loons Land 5

Common Loon 7

Loon Song 9

Call of the Loon 11

Wail 13

Tremolo 15

Hoots 17

Nesting 19

Hello World 21

Loon Chicks 23

Hitching a Ride 25

On Mama's Back 27

Fishing 29

Loon Party 31

Airborne 33

Loons Depart 35

Glossary 37

Resources 39

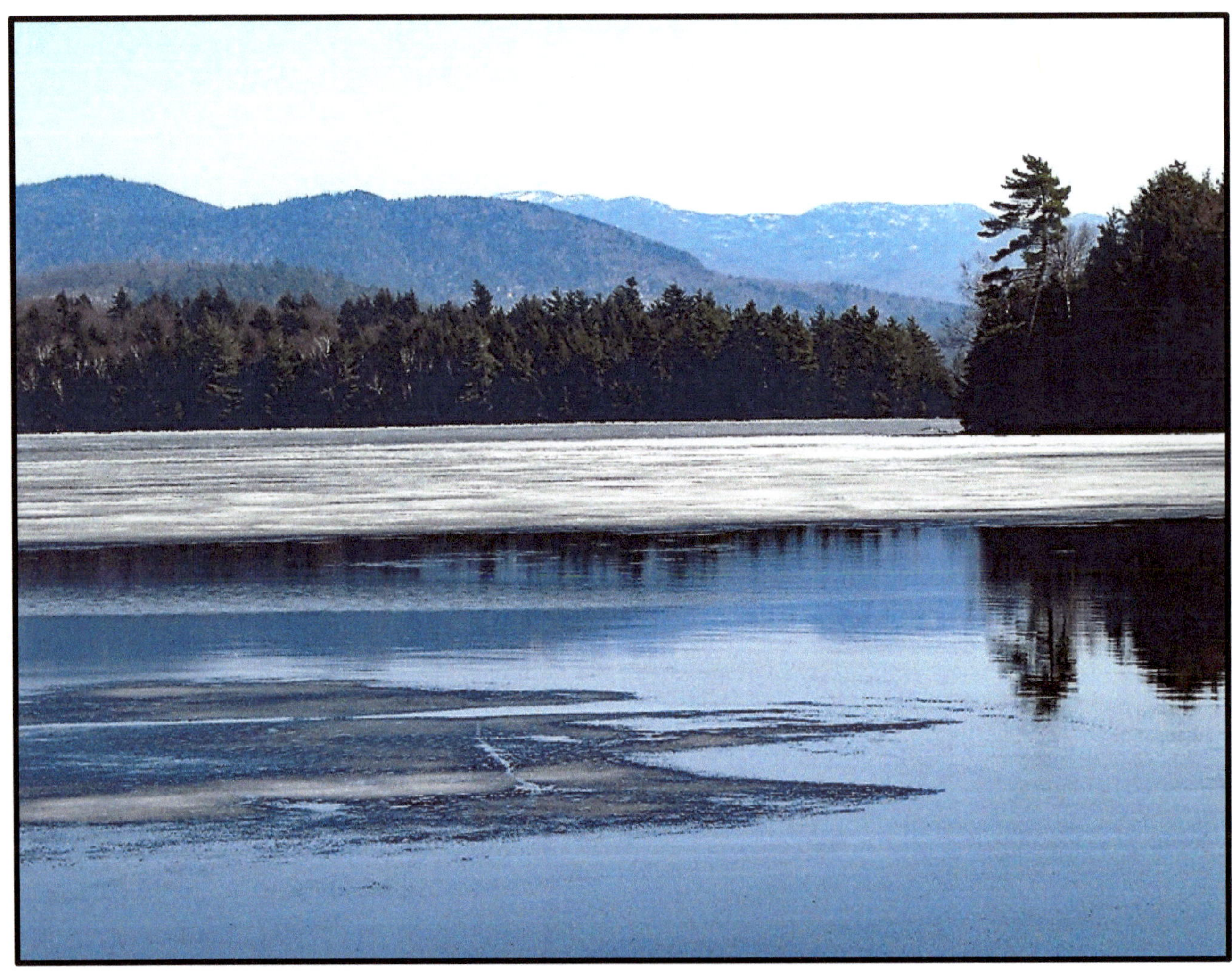

Waiting

Lake, still frozen.
Overhead, loons call.
Waiting.

Loons fly overhead looking for open water.
As soon as the lakes open, they descend.

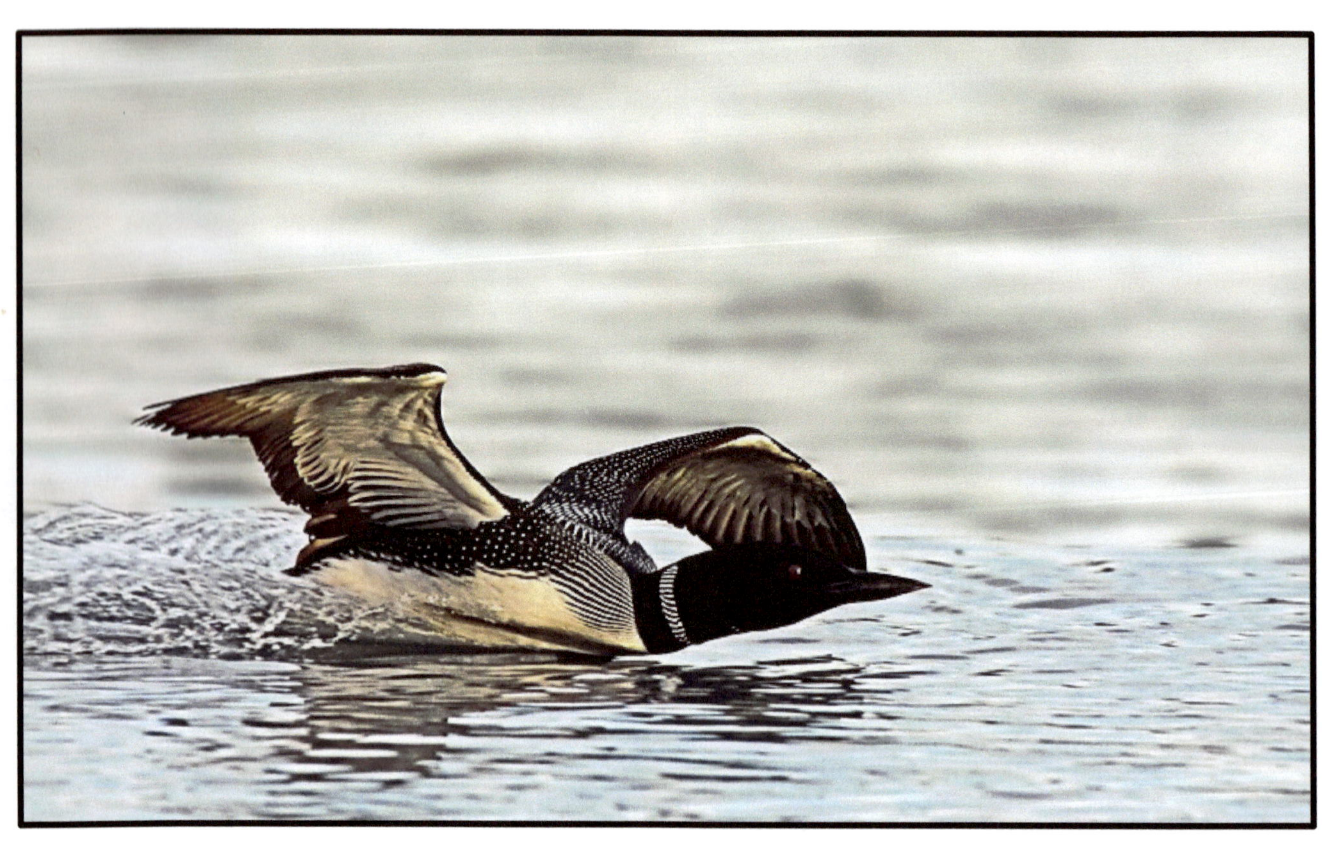

Loons Land

Ice is hard and snow is soft.
Loons appear, flying aloft.
Spring waits.

Frosty lakes crave wind and sun,
Ice turns gray and snow is done.
Lakes thaw.

As if waiting for the sight,
on chilly lakes loons alight.
Spring comes.

Flying low, long downward glide,
Touchdown hard on waters wide
Loons land!

Loons land when they see open water. They fly over the lake, gradually descending, their wings cupped towards their body and feet straight out behind them. They 'belly-slide' on the water with their breasts, moving at top speed and sending sprays of water high into the air. The landing is not graceful!

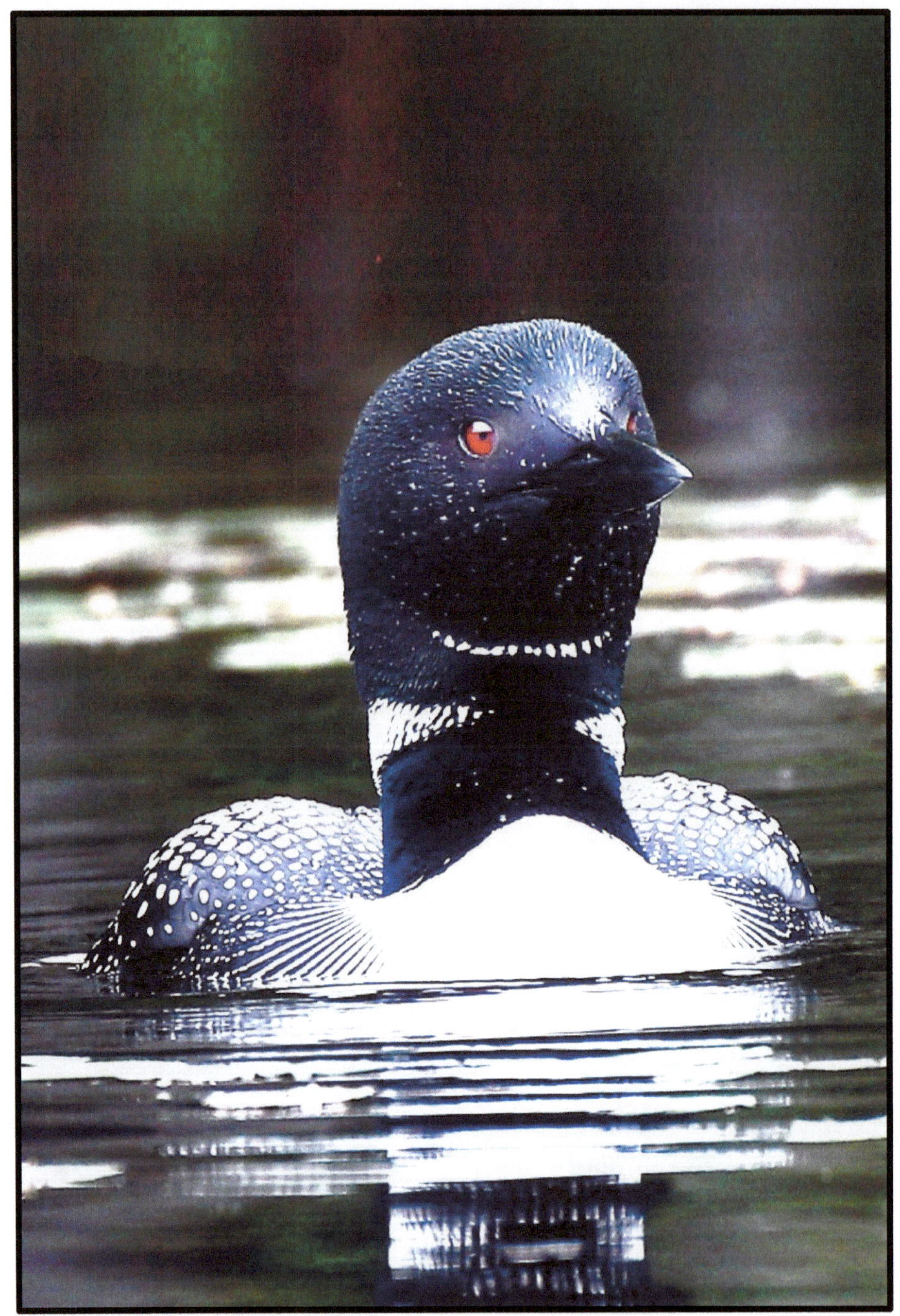

Common Loon

Have you heard?
No ordinary bird
that common loon.

The rise and fall
of their eerie call
wails, tremolos.

The ancient song
is loud and long
echoes on water.

Make no mistake,
he's King of the Lake,
that common loon.

There are 5 species of loons.

The _common loon_ is the most familiar. It breeds in the northern US and Canada. It is common in New England, the Adirondack lakes in northern New York State, and the Boundary Waters in Minnesota.

The _yellow-billed loon_ is the largest species. It breeds in the Arctic region and winters along the North Pacific Ocean's coasts and Norway's northwestern parts.

The _Pacific loon_ breeds in the tundra lakes of Alaska, Canada, and eastern Siberia, and winters on the Pacific coast.

The _black-throated loon_ is also known as the _Arctic loon_. It breeds in Alaska and northern Eurasia.

The _red-throated loon_ is the smallest of the loon species. It breeds in the Arctic regions of North America and Eurasia, and winters in the coastal waters of the northern areas.

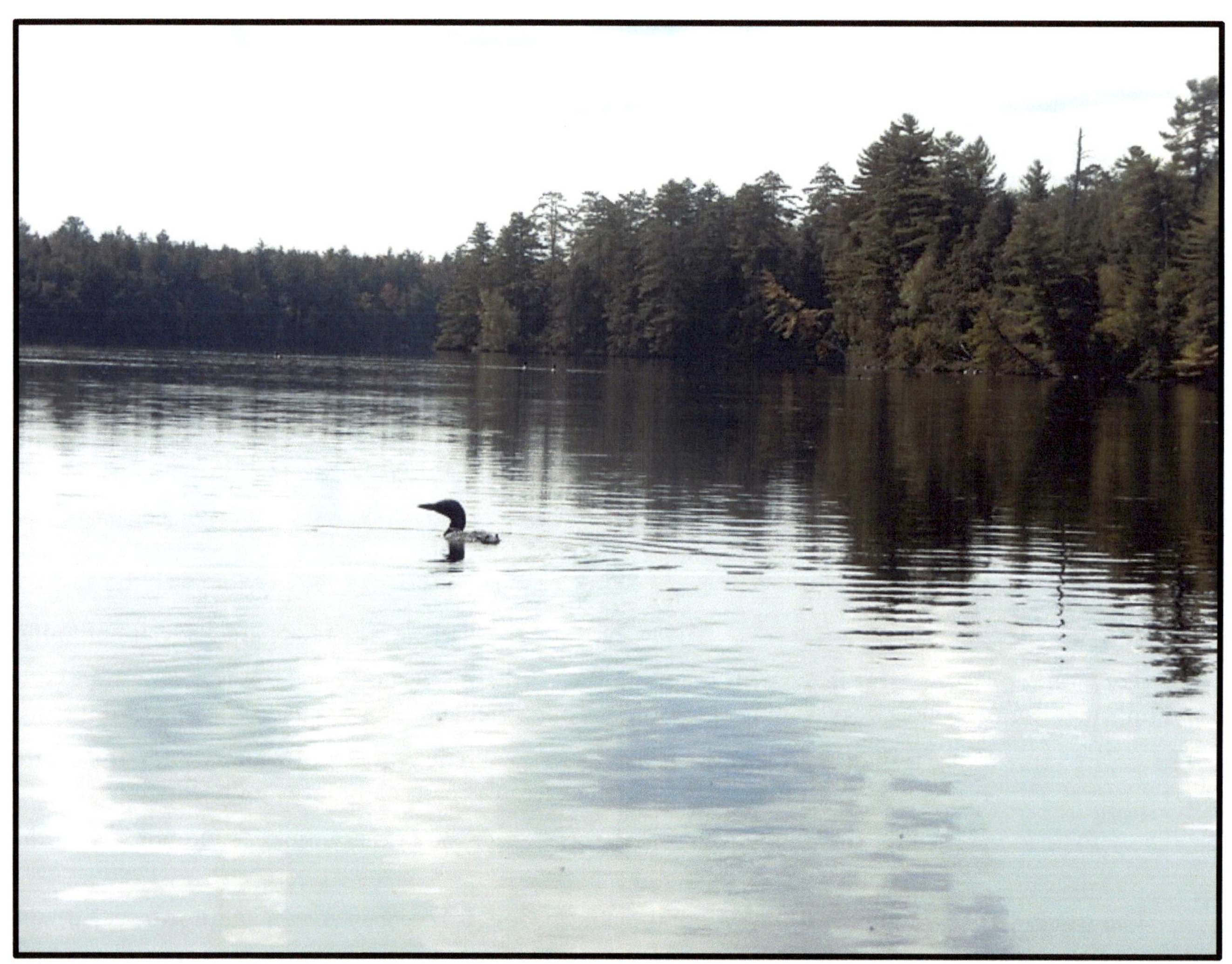

Loon Song

Loon calls loudly echo:
Wail, hoot, yodel, tremolo.
Wilderness silence.

There are four primary loon calls:

Hoots and peeps are short, single notes, used to keep in touch.
Young chicks will peep when calling parents and parents hoot in response.
A single loon will hoot softly when approaching another loon or a group of loons.

Wails are used to communicate a loon's location, as a loon wails when it is trying to find its mate or to let a flying loon overhead know it's on the water. They can be one, two or three notes.
Parents call the chicks with wails.

Yodels are loud, screeching territorial defense calls made only by males.
Each male loon has a slightly different, unique yodel.

Tremolos are very common calls. They sound like laughter, but they are the loon's warning about danger. As danger draws near, the sound becomes louder and more frequent.

Loons also use this call when flying over the territory of other loons. The in-flight tremolo is different from the one loons use when they are on the water—often higher-pitched.

Additionally, loons make a couple of softer calls:

A *soft mew* is made by members of a pair when they are courting or searching for a nest site.

Clucking is used by the parents to call the chicks.
It is only used during the first month after the chicks hatch.

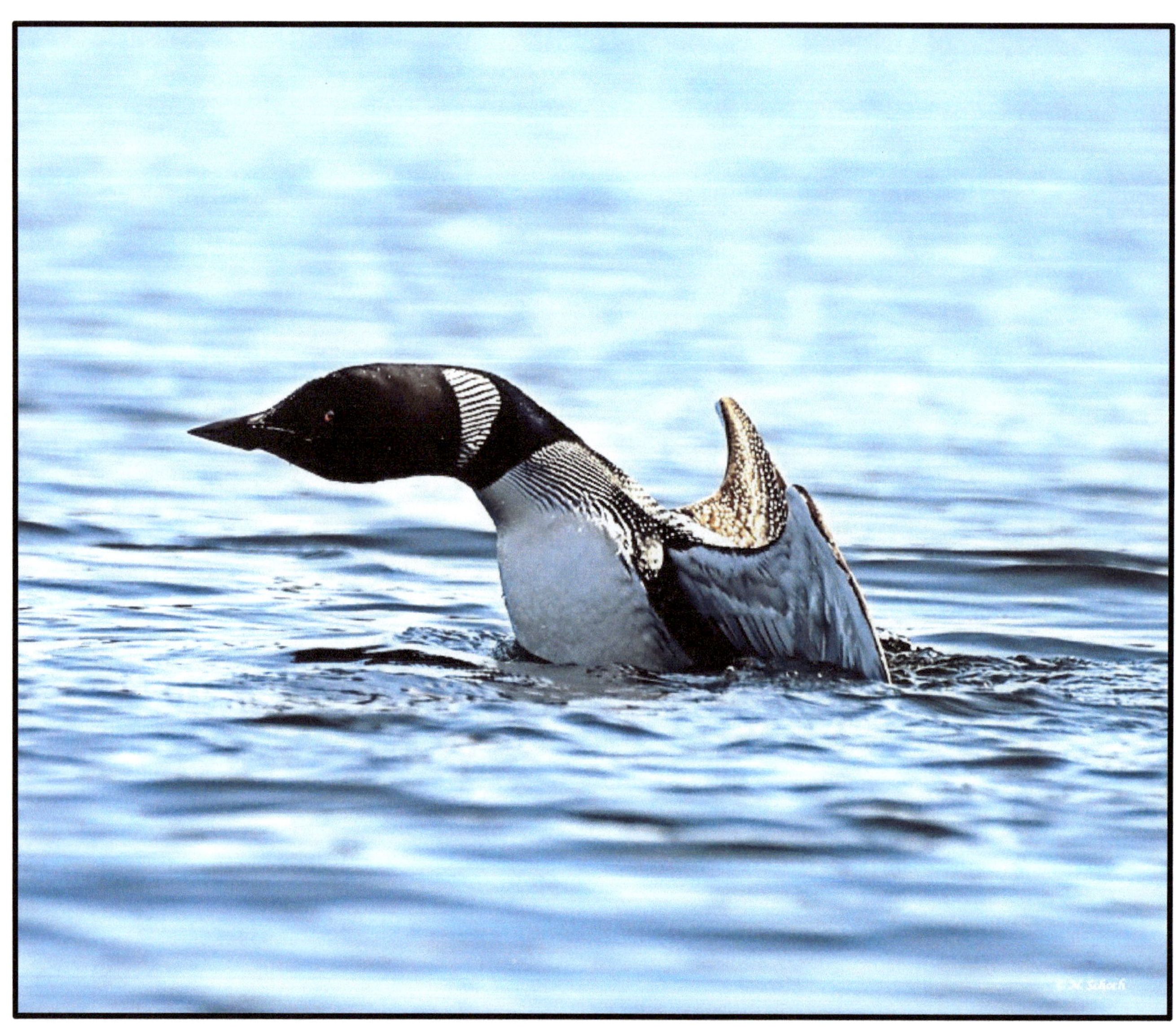

Call of the Loon

Listen! Night is quiet.
Then silence is broken
by a mournful sound.
Ooo Aaaaaaah Ooo.
Loud and low.

Danger! Keep out, invader!
Warning drifts across the lake—
yodel—pitch rises, falls.
Ooo Aaaaaaah Ooo.
Loud and low.

One loon calls to another—
primal, timeless sound.
Ancient echo of long ago.

Ooo Aaaaaaah Ooo.
Loud and low.

Wailing, desolate, drawn-out,
like lone wolf howls
echoing through the lake.
Ooo Aaaaaaah Ooo.
Loud and low.

Wild, ghostly night sound,
clear call of mournfulness—
loud sound of the wilderness:
Ooo Aaaaaaah Ooo.
Loud and low.

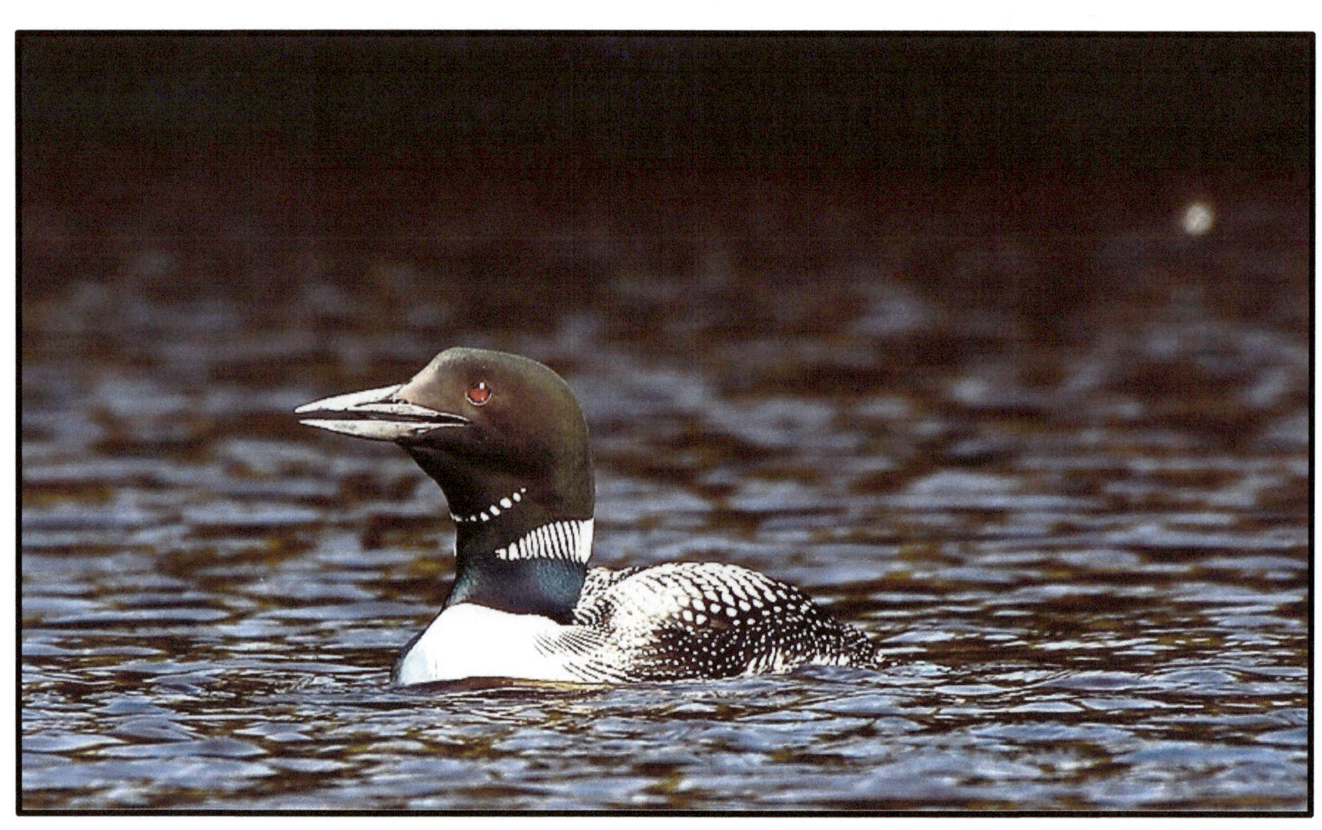

Wail

Listen to the howl
of the large waterfowl.
Stillness surrounds.

Loon's voice escalates,
reverberates, dissipates,
quieting all sounds.

The voice penetrates,
resonates, communicates:
danger surrounds.

Sounding a warning
this sunny morning:
Peril abounds.

Calling in fear:
Babies, stay near!
Don't swim around.

From the lagoon
the voice of the loon
quiets all sound.

A _wail_ sounds like a wolf howl.
It is used to call the mate, search for the chicks or warn the babies to stay close.

Technically, loons are waterbirds, not waterfowl.
Waterfowl is the name of a family of birds that includes ducks and geese, but not loons.

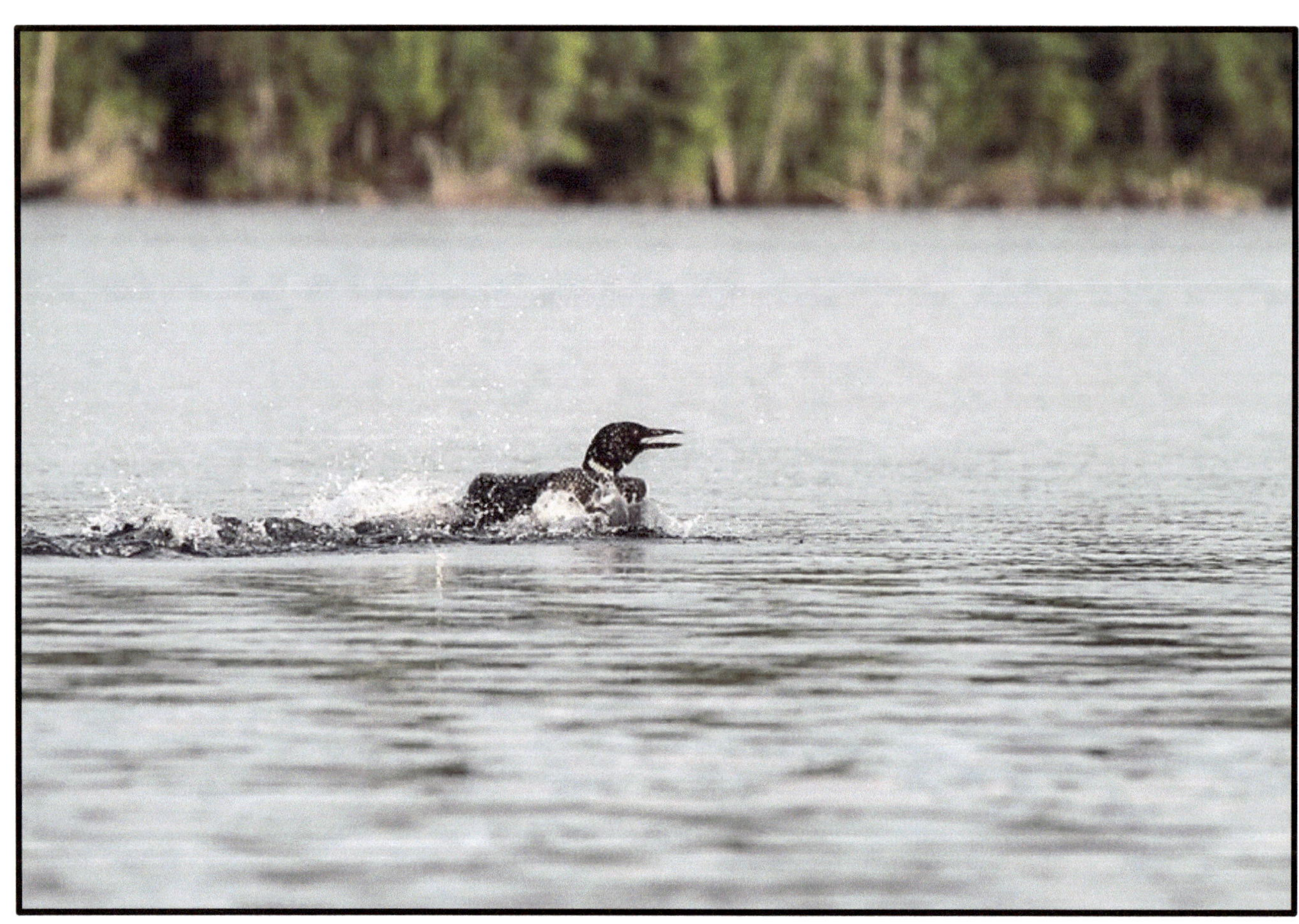

Tremolo

Off the lake rebounding,
through the woods resounding.

Loons come and loons go——
Wild laughing tremolo.

Joyful sound in the night
indicates a loon in flight.

Rising from water all around—
crazy person laughing sound.

Foreboding a time of woe,
peals out the ringing tremolo.

Laughter of the wilderness
tells of danger, speaks distress.

Peals out agony, cries out woe
startling, haunting tremolo.

Breaking evening silence,
full-toned, wild, intense,

Clear, loud, falsetto
tumultuous, throbbing tremolo.

Lake is calm, moon is bright—
laughter fades into the night.

The _tremolo_ is a very common call. It sounds like laughter, which is why the loon is sometimes called the "laughing duck" (though the loon is not a type of duck). But it's not laughter—it's a warning of imminent danger, such as an eagle flying overhead or another loon invading its territory.

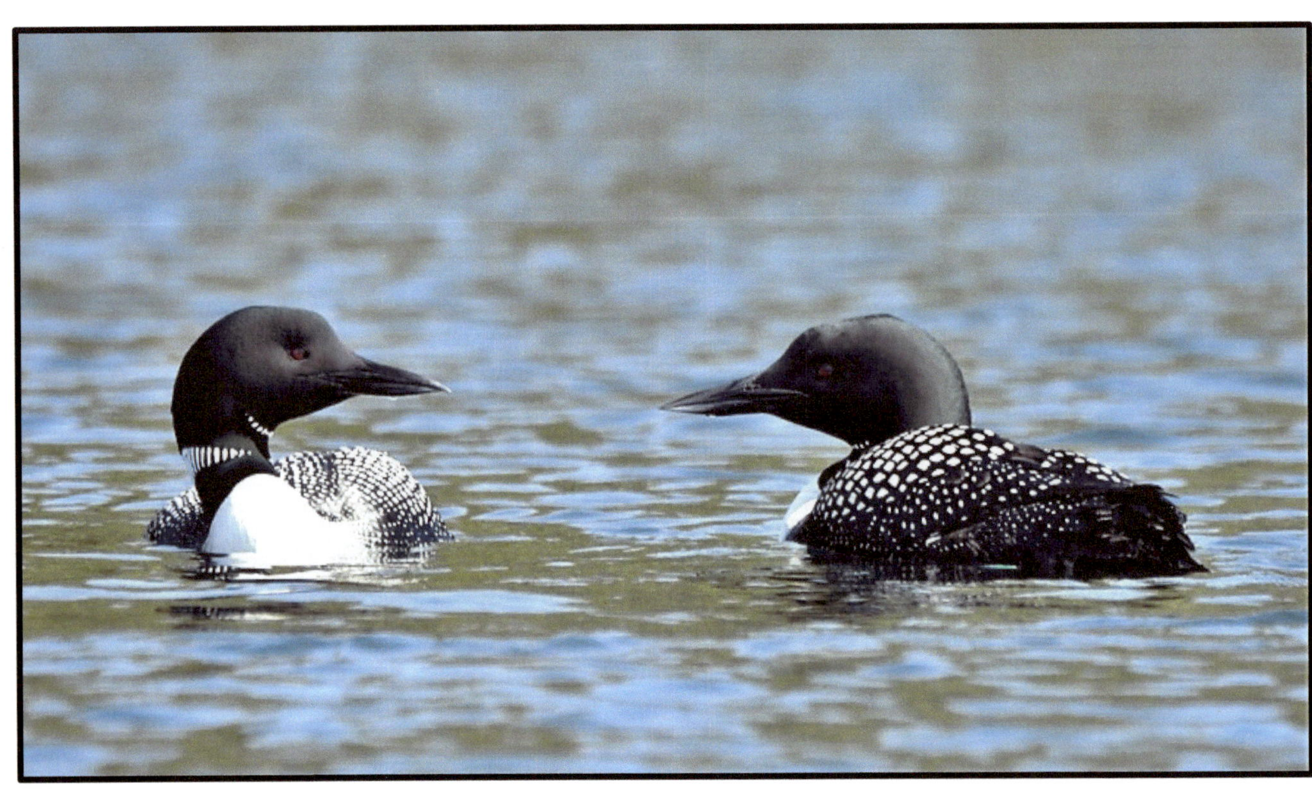

Hoots

On the lake, loons hoot,
chatting
with one another.

On the shore we walk,
talking,
listening to loons.

Hoots are soft, short, single notes loons use to communicate with one another.

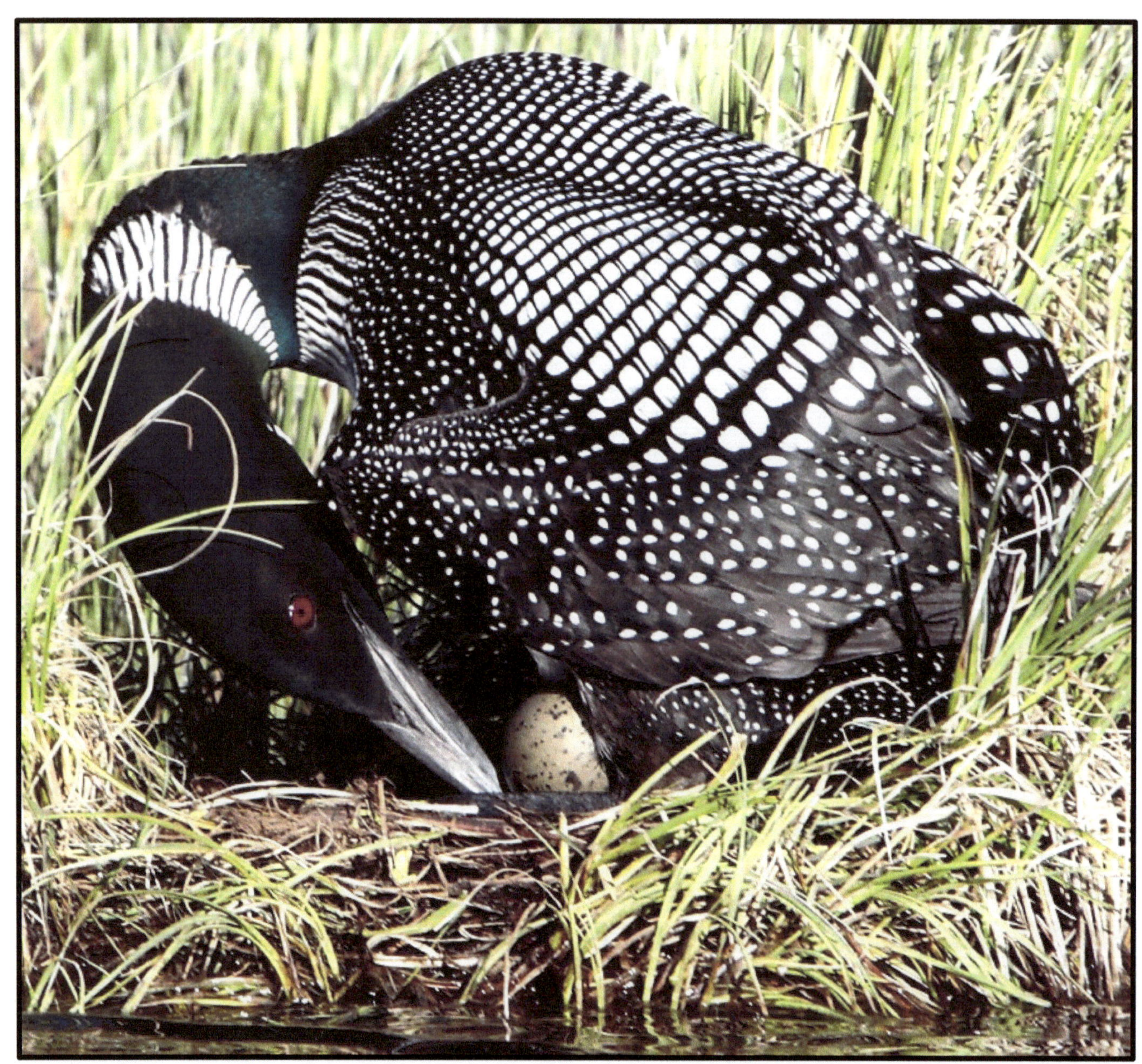

Loon Nest

Where, where shall we build our nest?
There, on the island, would be best.

Near to the water, safe from prey,
on an island or in a bay.

We will line it with grass and reeds,
soft and comfy for our needs.

A loon _nest_ is about 2 feet across. It looks like a clump of
dead grasses by the edge of the water.

Loons lay one or two eggs in the nest.
The tan oval eggs have numerous brown dots and are fairly large, 3-4 inches long.

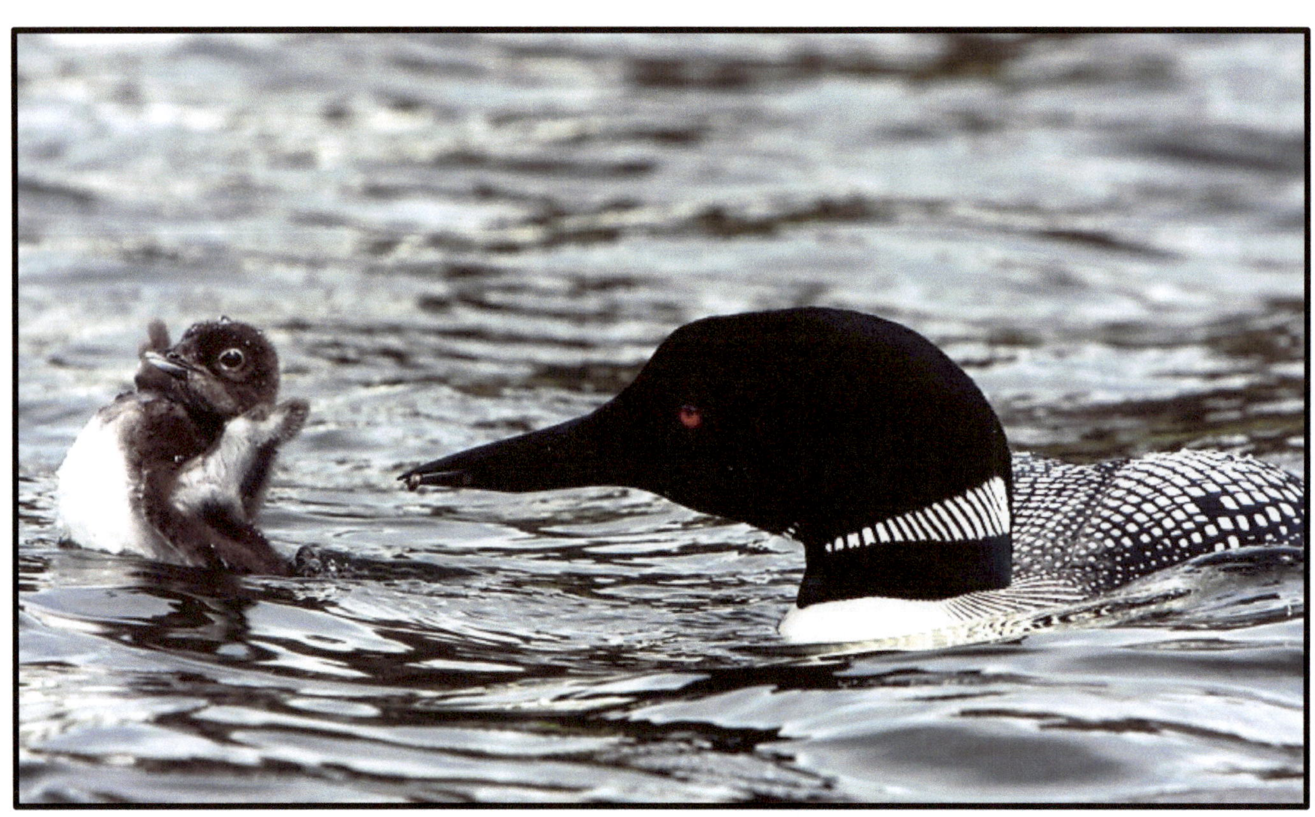

Hello World!

Peck, Peck, Peck!
Break the shell!

Peep, Peep, Peep.
All is well.

Make no sound.
Take a rest.

Look around
my grassy nest.

A loon _chick_ is about the size of a lemon when it's born.
It only spends a few hours in the nest, long enough to dry its fluffy, downy feathers.
A few hours after birth, the chicks slide into the water. They can swim soon after they hatch, although they spend a lot of time on their parents' backs when they're young. The nest is usually abandoned after the eggs hatch, but occasionally the loon family will revisit it off and on for a few days.

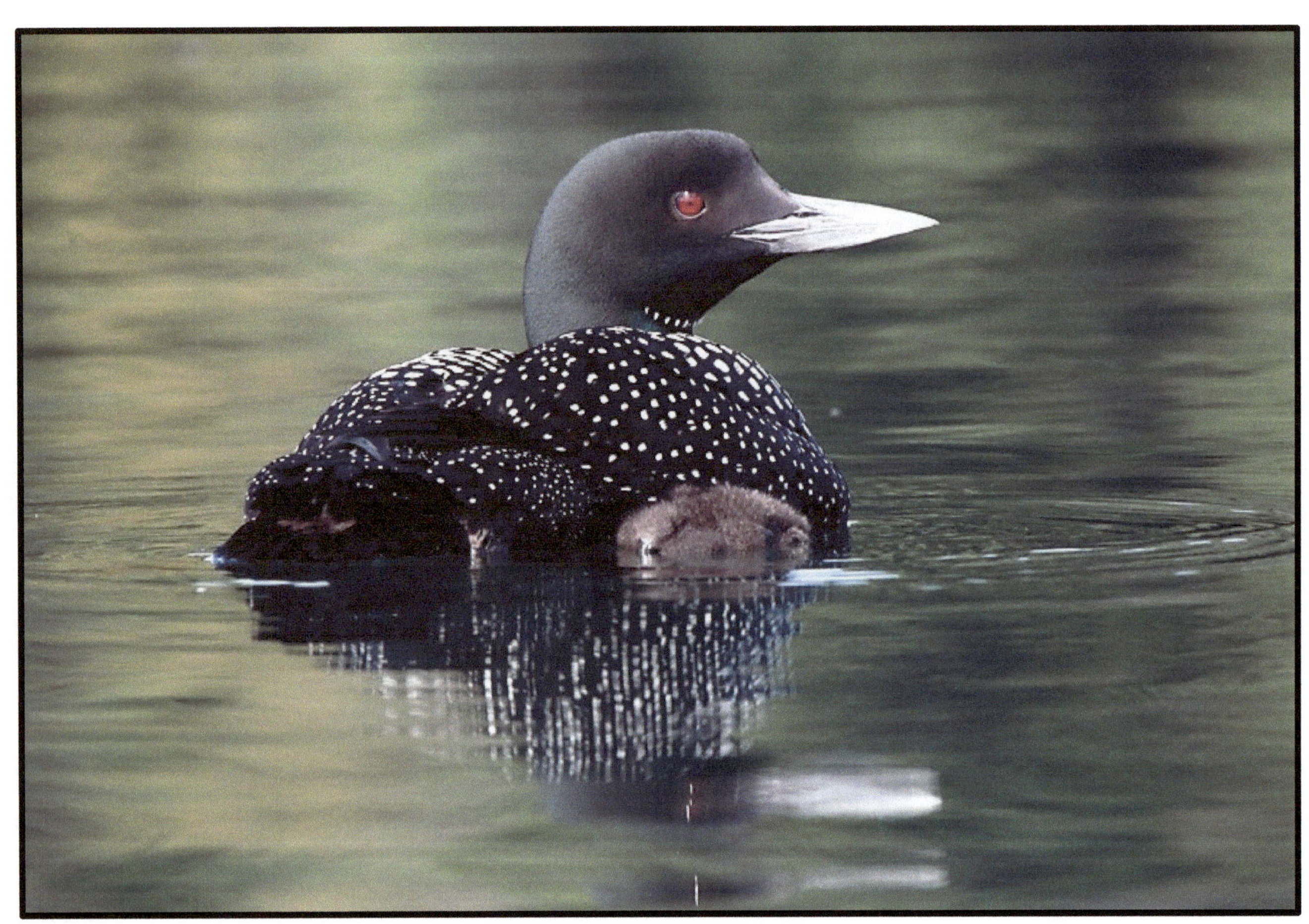

Loon Chicks

Chicks require continual care
like babies almost everywhere.

Parents bring them little fish.
Frogs and crayfish—so delish!

The chicks grow quick, and soon will be
swimming, diving quietly.

Loon chicks are pretty helpless. They cannot feed themselves. They rely on their parents to keep them safe and bring them fish, crayfish, and other critters to eat for the first one to two months. As they grow and can swim and dive better, they learn to catch their own fish.

Life is dangerous. They have to watch out for eagles, which hunt them from the air, and for snapping turtles, bass, and pike who try to catch them in the water.

Chicks grow very quickly, reaching 5-7 pounds by the time they are 10-12 weeks old.

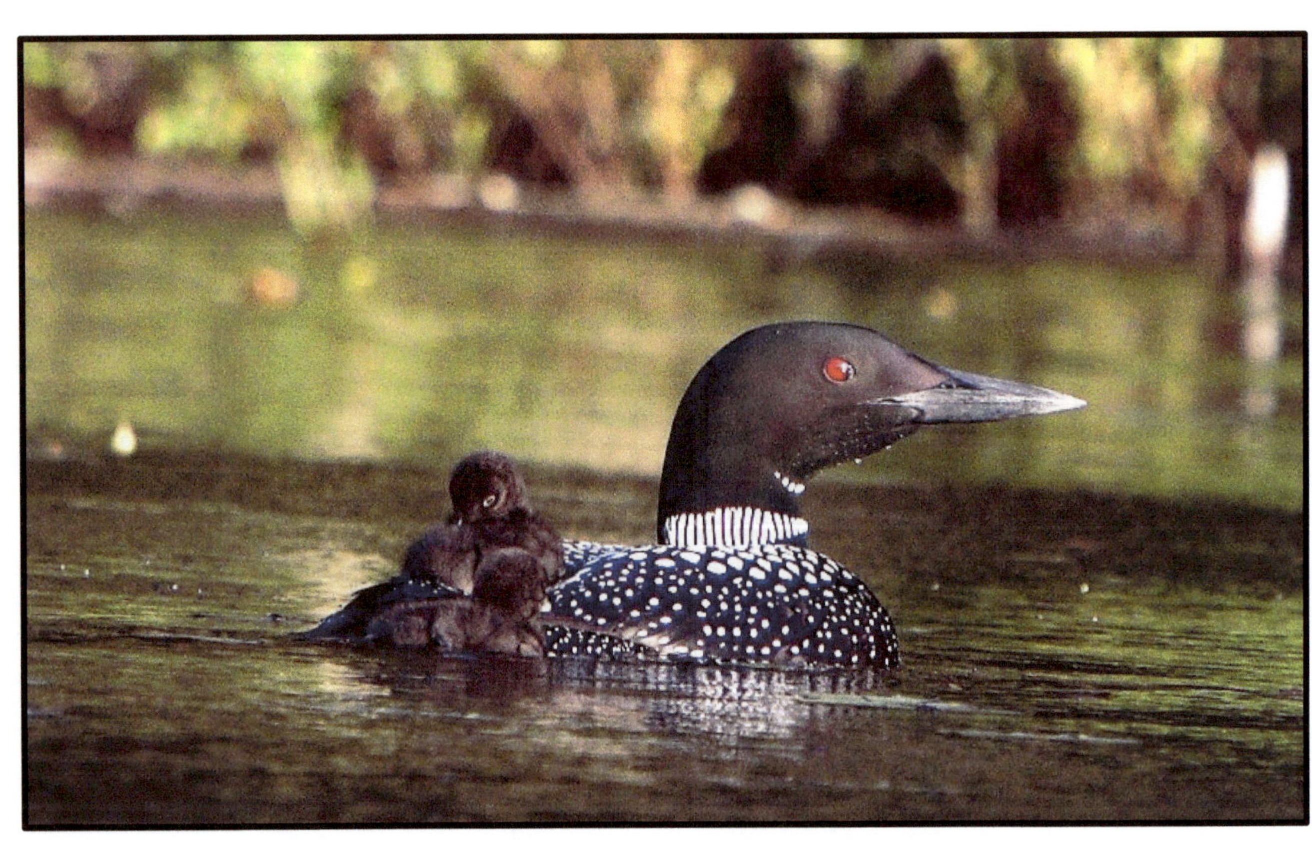

Hitching a Ride

Chicks sleep and rest, they have no lack
hitching a ride on mama's back.
Parents furnish every need
catching fish, their babies feed.

When they're tired, when they're cold
they do not need to be brave or bold.
Mama's back is so nearby
chicks climb up to lullaby.

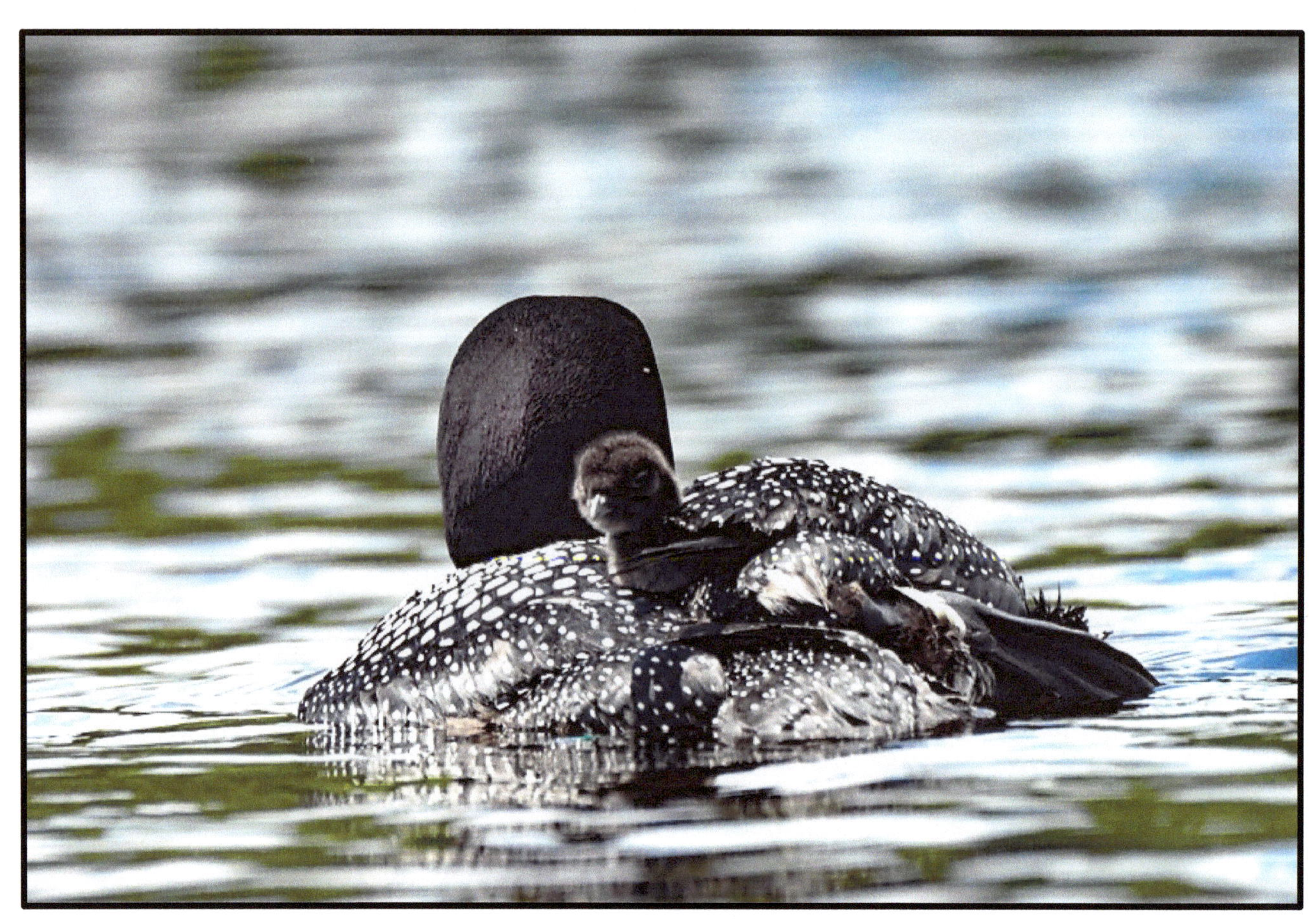

On Mama's Back

On Mama's back
I sit.
On Mama's back
I rest.
On Mama's back
I watch.
On Mama's back
I learn.
On Mama's back
I'm safe.

For the first two to three weeks of their life, loon chicks often ride on the parents' back.
As they grow, they ride less often, but may still ride when they need to nap, relax or dry out.

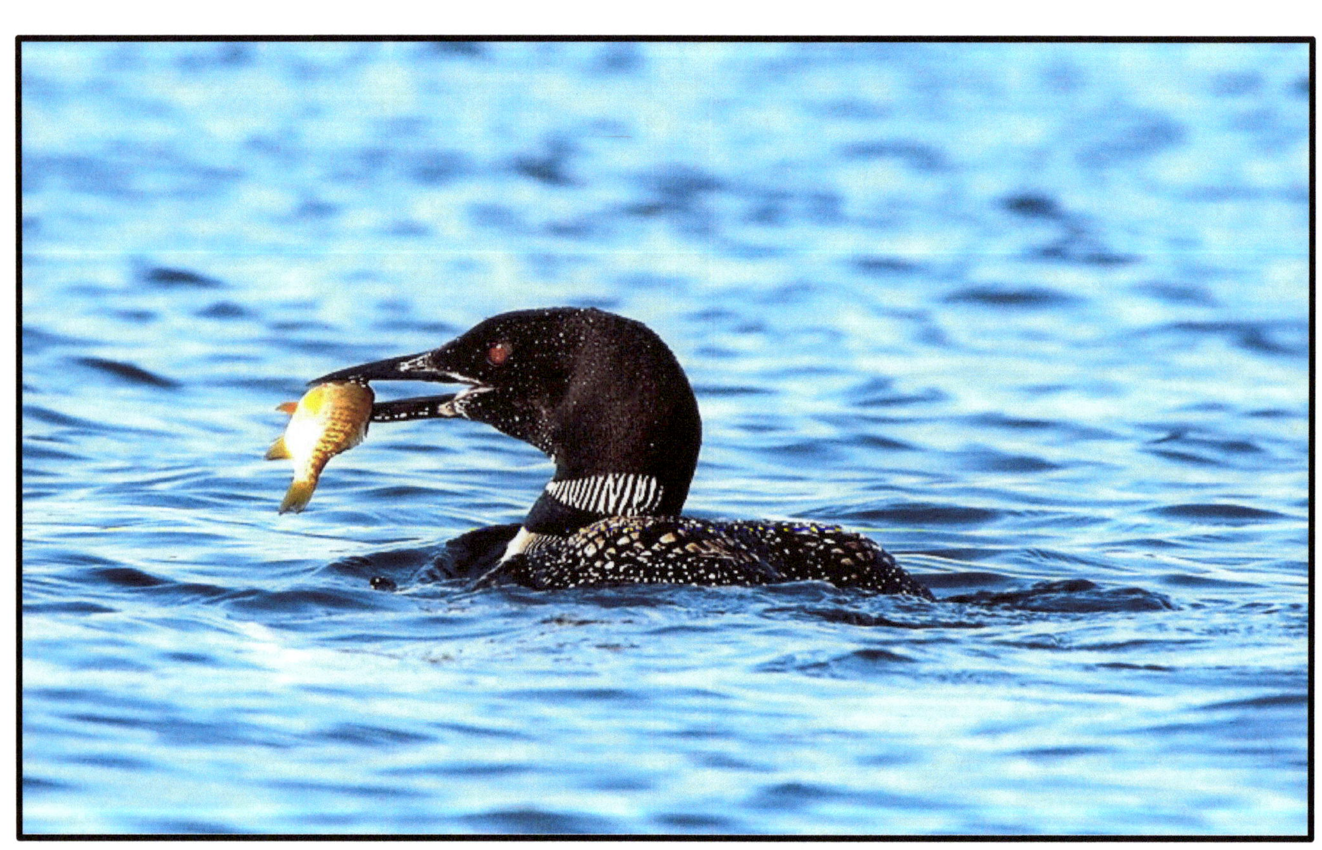

Fishing

In dark of night, loons fast asleep.
In bright of day, they dive down deep
in search of fish, frogs and snails
most swallowed whole, with heads and tails.

Other birds stand and wait;
they seem to watch and meditate.
But loons quickly chase and snatch
diving deep to grab their catch.

Loons spend their days fishing for food. They eat mainly fish, but also other creatures like frogs, leeches, snails and crayfish. When you see loons diving, it is usually to catch fish or hunt for food.

Loons peer underwater and move their heads from side to side to locate prey.

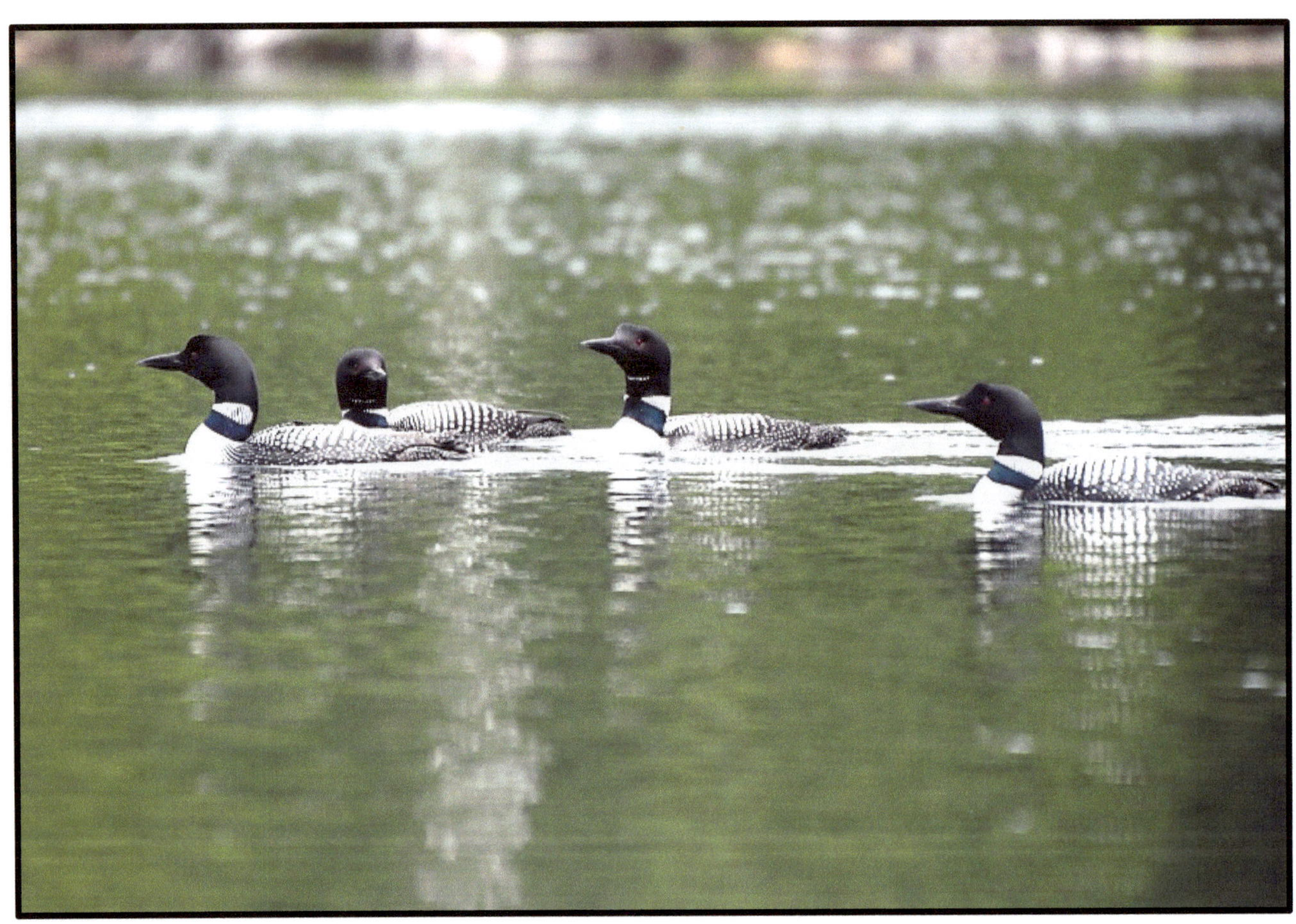

Loon Party

Loons arrive,
two, three, five…
then, they dive.

Let's party!

Flocking together,
in any weather,
preen a feather.

Let's party!

Residents greet
visitors sweet.
Let us meet!

Party's On!

Wings flapping,
water slapping,
not napping.

Party On!

After an hour,
fun turns sour.
Loons are dour.

Party's over!

Waters splatter
as loons scatter.
No matter.

Party's over!

Waters foam.
Loons who roam
fly back home.

Goodbye!

In late summer and throughout the fall, loons become very social, gather together in groups and appear to enjoy each other's company. They may form a circle and dip their bills and heads into the water in a ritual behavior.

Scientists believe loons do this to get ready for their migration and reinforce their collaborative feeding rituals. These gatherings build relationships and cooperation among mature loons. Adults leave the young loons to fend for themselves when they socialize with other loons. Adults migrate about a month before young loons.

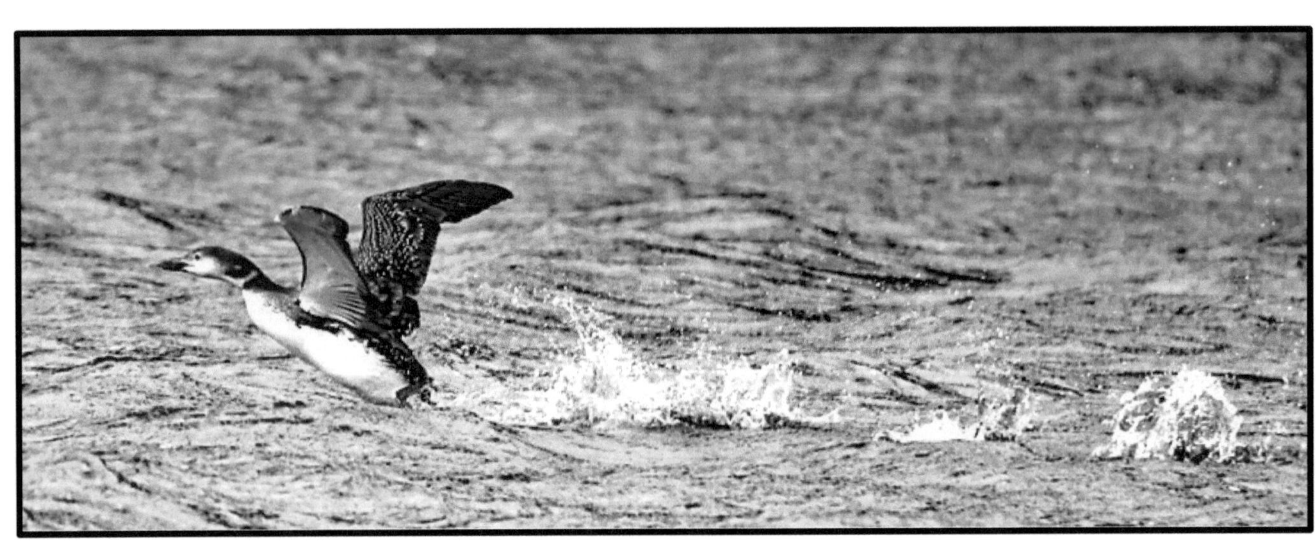

Airborne

Wings tap, tap, tap
quickly rap
on the water.

    Loon prances, dances,
    struggling to rise
    into the skies
    from the water.

        Quicken gait, accelerate.
        Flapping away
        on lake's runway
        off the water.

            Away they fly
            into the sky.

            Goodbye.

Taking off from the water is hard for loons. Their bodies are large and heavy. They run on the water, into the wind for up to a quarter-mile—four football fields—to get enough lift to get airborne. They seem to teeter-totter on the water, beating their wings furiously as they run until they're able to gain enough speed and lift to rise up and fly.

Once airborne, they fly at about the same speed as a car on a highway—60 to 70 miles per hour. They can fly for hours non-stop when they are migrating. One loon with an implanted satellite transmitter made the trip from the Adirondack Mountains of northern New York State to the Atlantic coast in less than 8 hours! Research on common loon migration has provided us with valuable data about where loons spend the winter, which will help to paint a clearer picture of the conservation concerns that impact common loons throughout the year.

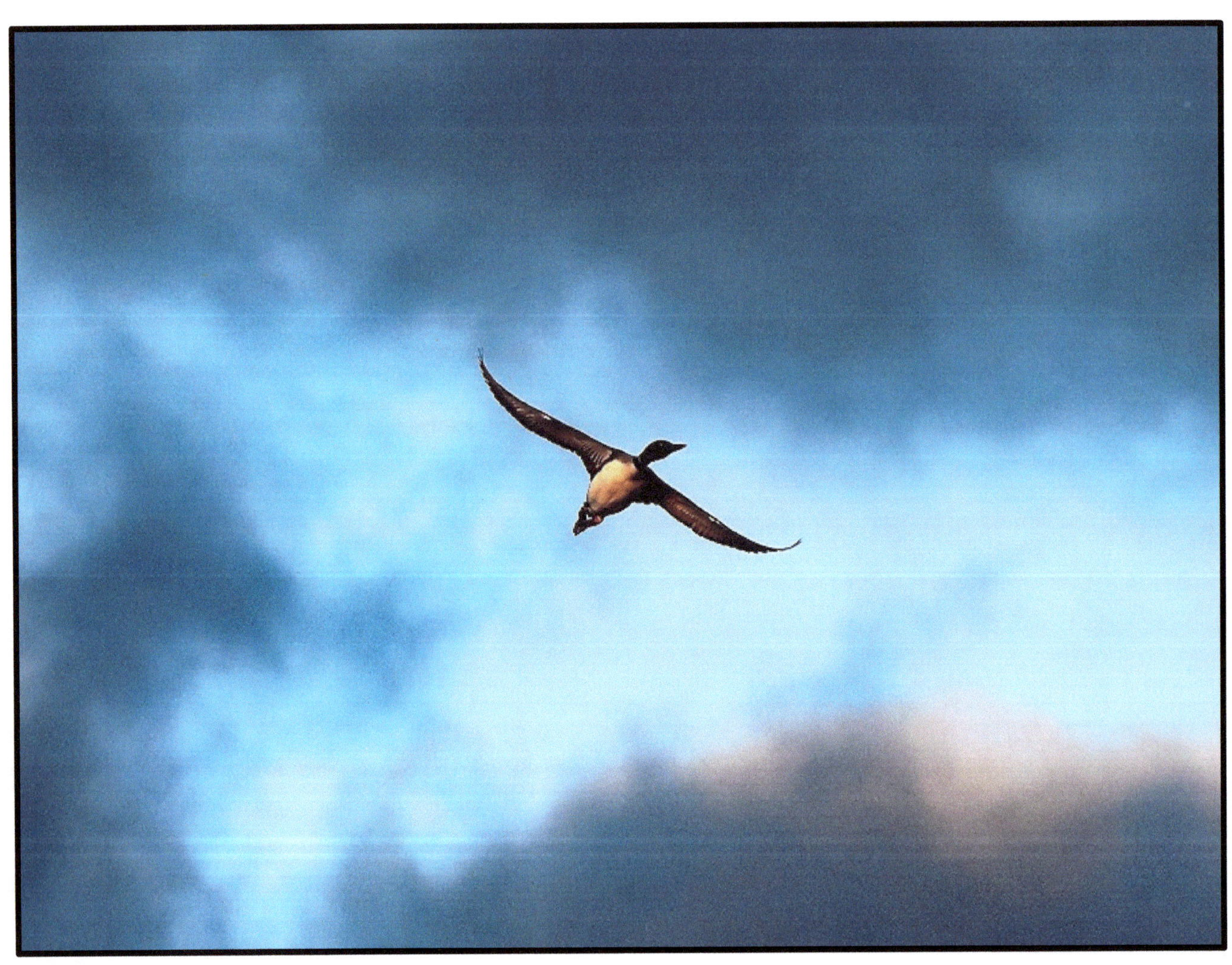

Loons Depart

When ice forms, loons must flee
for the ocean, for the sea.

Before lakes freeze, they must depart.
Single birds have an early start.

Adult loons leave in September.
Younger birds wait till November.

Lifting off, like a plane
is important; they can't remain.

On ice-filled lakes they would die,
so to the ocean they must fly.

Ocean water doesn't freeze,
so the loons can swim with ease.

Like a raincoat, the loon's feather
is warm and snug in wintry weather.

Though north winds blow, and water's chill,
it will not harm them, it will not kill.

As lakes start to ice over in late fall, loons depart. They have to find open water where they can still hunt for fish.

Adults leave first; the chicks follow a few weeks later. Adult loons usually fly directly to their winter territories, while young birds may stop at the first open water they find and move south as lakes freeze.

Loons go to the ocean or to large reservoirs in the south. They stay there till spring, often feeding in groups. They are not interested in defending a territory when not breeding, so they rarely use territorial calls.

With their thick waterproof plumage, cold temperatures and north winds don't seem to bother them. A lake icing over is the trap they have to avoid. Unfortunately, late-hatched juveniles or injured adults who are unable to fly await a slow death.

Loons from the Northeast migrate from freshwater northern lakes to saltwater seas in the Atlantic Ocean or the Gulf of Mexico. They are specially adapted to switch between fresh and saltwater and have special glands near their eyes that excrete excess salt.

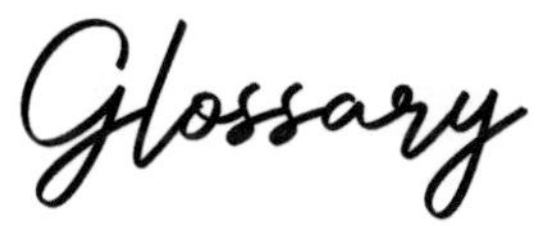

Glossary

Breed – to raise young

Chick – a baby bird

Camouflage – blending into the surroundings so as not to be seen by predators

Down – soft, fluffy feathers

Habitat – place where the bird lives

Hatch – to break out of an egg

Hoot – a loon call that consists of soft, short, single notes, used to communicate

Incubate – to keep eggs warm

Loon chick – a baby loon

Mate – a partner of the opposite sex; a male or female loon

Mating – a male and female joining together to breed

Markings – distinctive features

Migrate – to travel from one territory to another, usually in spring and fall to reach food or mating grounds

Molting – shedding of feathers before growing new ones

Nest – a structure of grasses, twigs and mud where birds lay and incubate their eggs, and some birds raise their young

Nesting site – a place to build a nest

Plumage – bird feathers

Predator – animal that preys on, or hunts, other animals

Preening, preen gland – an organ that produces oil used by the bird to oil and clean its feathers

Ritual – an established or specific routine, pattern or procedure

Streamlined – smooth, sleek shape

Territory – home area defended against intruders and predators

Tremolo – a loon call that sounds like laughter, but is used to warn of danger

Trespass – to go into another's territory

Webbed feet – feet with skin stretched between toes

Wail – a long one, two– or three-note loon call used to call the mate or the chicks to come closer

Yodel – a loon call made by a male loon when claiming their territory

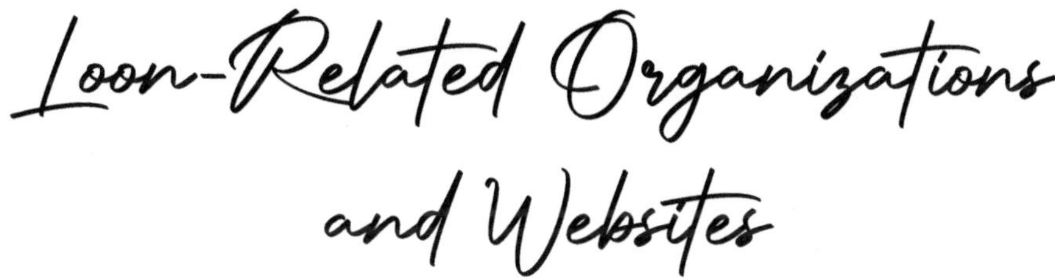

Loon-Related Organizations and Websites

- Adirondack Center for Loon Conservation: www.adkloon.org

- Biodiversity Research Institute: www.briwildlife.org

- Canadian Lakes Loon Survey: www.birdscanada.org/volunteer/clls/

- Cornell's Lab of Ornithology: www.birds.cornell.edu

- Journey North: https://journeynorth.org/loon/index.html

- Loon Preservation Committee: www.loon.org

- Loon Watch: www.northland.edu/sustainability/soei/loonwatch/

- The Maine Loon Project: https://maineaudubon.org/projects/loons/

- Michigan Loon Preservation Association: www.michiganloons.com

- Minnesota Dept. of Natural Resources' Common Loon page: www.dnr.state.mn.us/birds/commonloon.html

- Montana Loon Society: www.montanaloons.org

- Vermont Loon Conservation Project: https://vtecostudies.org/projects/lakes-ponds/common-loon-conservation/

About Atmosphere Press

Atmosphere Press is an independent, full-service publisher for excellent books in all genres and for all audiences. Learn more about what we do at atmospherepress.com.

We encourage you to check out some of Atmosphere's latest releases, which are available at Amazon.com and via order from your local bookstore:

Until the Kingdom Comes, poetry by Jeanne Lutz

Warcrimes, poetry by GOODW.Y.N

The Freedom of Lavenders, poetry by August Reynolds

Convalesce, poetry by Enne Zale

Poems for the Bee Charmer (And Other Familiar Ghosts), poetry by Jordan Lentz

Serial Love: When Happily Ever After… Isn't, poetry by Kathy Kay

Flowers That Die, poetry by Gideon Halpin

Through The Soul Into Life, poetry by Shoushan B

Embrace The Passion In A Lover's Dream, poetry by Paul Turay

Reflections in the Time of Trumpius Maximus, poetry by Mark Fishbein

Drifters, poetry by Stuart Silverman

As a Patient Thinks about the Desert, poetry by Rick Anthony Furtak

Winter Solstice, poetry by Diana Howard

Blindfolds, Bruises, and Break-Ups, poetry by Jen Schneider

Songs of Snow and Silence, poetry by Jen Emery

INHABITANT, poetry by Charles Crittenden

Godless Grace, poetry by Michael Terence O'Brien

March of the Mindless, poetry by Thomas Walrod

In the Village That Is Not Burning Down, poetry by Travis Nathan Brown

Mud Ajar, poetry by Hiram Larew

About the Artists

Yvona Fast has published poems, recipes, articles and several books. Her poetry chapbooks include *Adirondack Blue Seasons* (Dark Particle, 2018), *Adirondack Seasons: Haiku* (Local Gems, 2020), and *Different* (Foothills, 2017). For more information, visit her website, www.yvonafast.com. She loves nature, and can be found hiking, snowshoeing or cross-country skiing in woods and paddling on lakes.

Dr. Nina Schoch has been studying loons in New York's Adirondack Park since 1998 and is the Executive Director of the Adirondack Center for Loon Conservation, www.adkloon.org. She greatly enjoys documenting the behavior of animals through her photographs, as the camera captures movements that are too fast to see with one's eyes. A veterinarian, Dr. Schoch is also a wildlife rehabilitator and a member of numerous wildlife health organizations. She spends her free time exploring nature on foot or by canoe to watch loons and other wildlife.

www.ingramcontent.com/pod-product-compliance
Lightning Source LLC
Chambersburg PA
CBHW042154030726
47599CB00004B/726